DOES IT ALWAYS SNOW IN CANADA?

GEOGRAPHY 4TH GRADE
CHILDREN'S CANADA BOOKS

Speedy Publishing LLC

40 E. Main St. #1156

Newark, DE 19711

www.speedypublishing.com

Copyright 2017

In this book, we're going to talk about exploring the country of **CANADA**.
So, let's get right to it!

WHERE IS CANADA?

Canada is part of North America and is in the Northern Hemisphere. The southern border of Canada is right next to the northern border of the United States. The dividing line between the two countries goes right through the Great Lakes. Greenland is north of Canada and the state of Alaska borders Canada at its northwestern edge.

MAP OF CANADA

WHAT ARE THE GEOGRAPHIC AND NATURAL FEATURES OF CANADA?

Canada is the largest country in terms of landmass in North America. Its area covers almost 10 million square kilometers or almost 4 million square miles. In fact, Canada is so massive that it stretches out over six different time zones!

After Russia it is the country with the largest landmass in the world. Much of Canada's terrain is forested wilderness that isn't populated. Only about 1/2% of the world's population, about 36 million people, live in Canada compared to the 323 million who live in the United States.

Canada has a rugged terrain with tall, majestic mountains and densely forested valleys. It has hilly regions of plains and pristine lakes and rivers. It's a country of great natural beauty.

Canada has some of the oldest rocks on the face of planet Earth. These rocks are part of a hilly region of land called the Canadian Shield, also known as the Laurentian Plateau. This area of swamps and lakes stretches across the northern region of Canada and surrounds Hudson Bay.

LAURENTIAN PLATEAU

It is composed of igneous and metamorphic rocks that came from ancient volcanic activity. Some of the rocks there are over 4 billion years old.

At the country's northern border lies the Arctic region. Glaciers, ice, and snow cover this part of the country and it is very cold. Even though the environment in this region is harsh, the First Nations people, also called the Native Canadians, live here. They survive by hunting and fishing.

NATIVE CANADIANS

OTTERS HOLDING HANDS

Because Canada has so much dense forest wilderness, it is home to many different species of mammals. Bears, mountain lions, wolves, and deer roam in its forests. Beavers make dams in its rivers and otters are found in its waterways. Bighorn sheep and rabbits graze in its meadows.

Canada has so many rivers and lakes that it contains one-fifth of the fresh water on the planet. The rivers have abundant populations of salmon as well as trout.

MUSK OXEN

Herds of American buffalo as well as pronghorn antelope run across the southern grasslands. In the northern part of the country there are moose in the expansive evergreen forests. Black bears can be found there too. In the frozen north, reindeer as well as musk ox are at home in the arctic tundra.

WHAT IS THE CULTURE LIKE IN CANADA?

Canada's culture has been influenced by the cultures of Britain and France as well as the cultures of the native peoples who lived there before the Europeans came. Both English and French are spoken in Canada. There are also immigrants from other countries who have settled in Canada and their cultures have blended with the existing culture and become mainstream.

LEIF ERIKSSON

WHAT IS THE HISTORY OF CANADA?

At one time there was land that connected the continent of Asia and the continent of North America. The very first people who came to Canada crossed that "land bridge" somewhere between 15,000 to 30,000 years ago. Around 1000 AD, the famous Viking, Leif Eriksson sailed to Newfoundland in Canada. He tried to start a settlement there, but the environment was incredibly harsh so people didn't stay.

Both the French and the British set foot in Canada during the 16th Century. These two countries were always fighting. Further conflicts between farmers and the trappers who made their living from furs led to a series of wars beginning in 1689 and ending in 1763. The last of these wars was called the French and Indian War. The British were victorious and gained control over the country, but the French remained a powerful force in certain regions and still have an influence today.

FRENCH AND INDIAN WAR

About half of the people who live in Canada are descended from the original British and French settlers. Other European immigrants as well as immigrants from countries in Asia make up the multicultural mix. The native peoples compose about 4% of the country's population.

Canada became an independent country in 1931. It has had many boundary changes over the years, but today it is composed of ten different provinces as well as three territories.

WHAT PLACES ARE GOOD FOR EXPLORING IN CANADA?

There are so many exciting places to go in Canada. Here are just a few places you might like to visit.

DINOSAUR PROVINCIAL PARK IN ALBERTA

Do you love studying and digging up dinosaur bones? Then, you will love the Dinosaur Provincial Park in Alberta. It's actually one of the largest fossil beds of dinosaurs in the entire world. It's so important to paleontologists that it's been named a UNESCO heritage site.

DINOSAUR PROVINCIAL PARK

ROYAL TYRRELL MUSEUM

  The fossils that have been excavated there include about 500 different animal species and 40 species of dinosaurs.

  About two hours away is the Royal Tyrrell Museum, which is located in Drumheller, Alberta. You can dig up bones that are still in the ground if you visit the Fossil Discovery Center. You can also watch paleontologists at work on some fossil specimens.

THE AURORA BOREALIS

Are you excited about natural wonders in the sky? Then, you will want to witness the aurora borealis at night. It is one of the most beautiful natural wonders in the world. Charged particles collide with atmospheric gases to create a dazzling display of gold, red, and green lights. You can see the aurora borealis, also called the Northern Lights, from the Yukon, Nunavit, and Northwest Territories of Canada.

AURORA BOREALIS

THE CN TOWER IN TORONTO

Do you enjoy the view from the top of tall buildings? Then, you might enjoy going to the top of the CN Tower, which is the tallest structure in the city of Toronto. It has a glass floor that allows you to look straight down to the ground below. There's also a theater that shows you a film about how the tower was constructed.

QUEBEC CITY IN QUEBEC

Do you like winter sports like skiing? Then, you may want to visit the city of Québec. The people of Québec love the winter season and they are not afraid to show it! In addition to skiing, there are sports such as snow tubing and canoeing in icy water. French is spoken in Québec and the food is inspired by French cuisine too!

QUEBEC CITY

NIAGARA FALLS

Do you find waterfalls exciting? Then, you may want to visit Niagara Falls in Ontario, Canada. The falls are about an hour drive from the city of Toronto. Once you are there, you can see these spectacular falls at a very close distance from the top's edge. Another exciting place to visit in Niagara Falls is Marineland where there are shows with marine mammals such as killer whales, beluga whales, and dolphins.

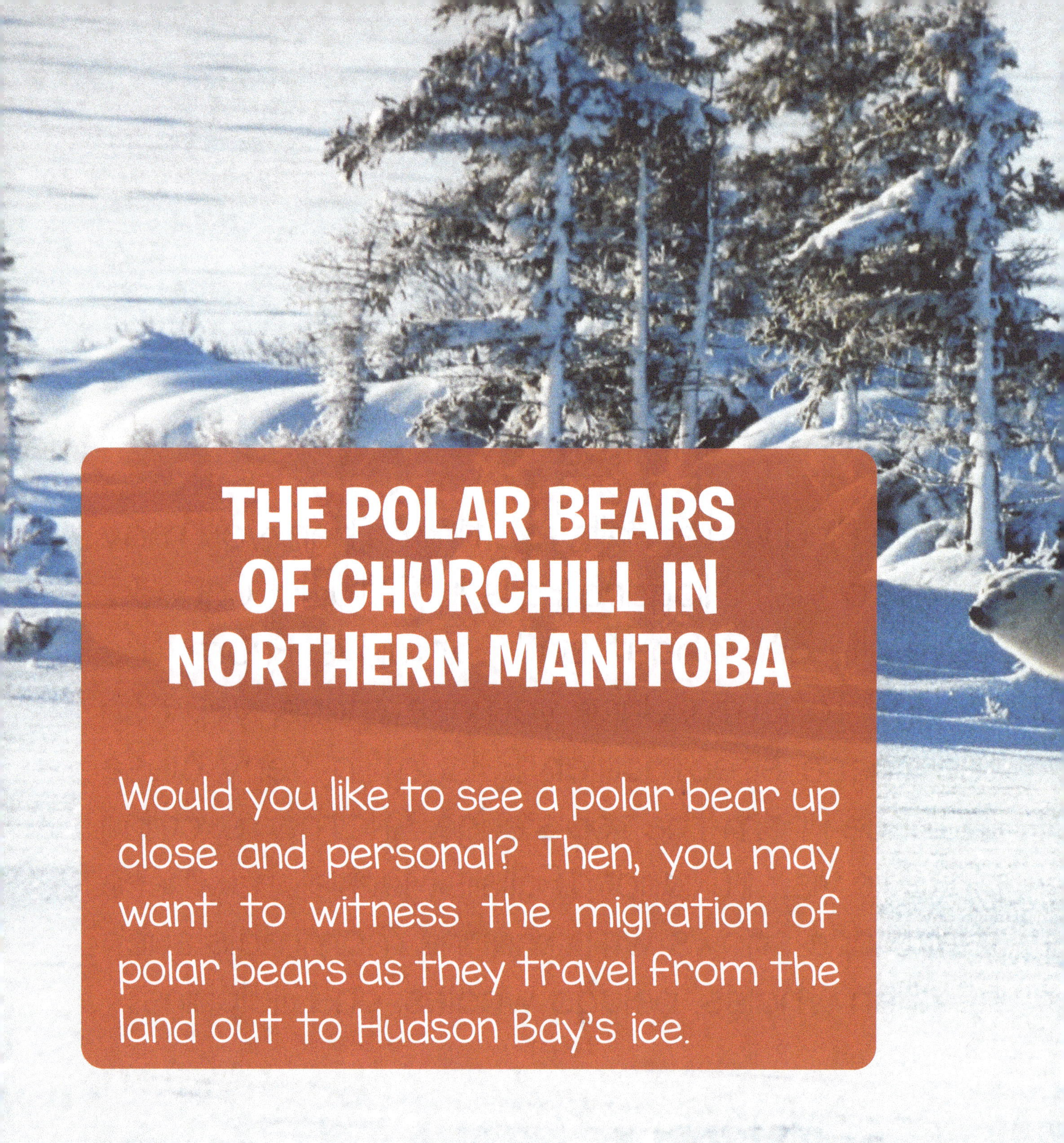

THE POLAR BEARS OF CHURCHILL IN NORTHERN MANITOBA

Would you like to see a polar bear up close and personal? Then, you may want to witness the migration of polar bears as they travel from the land out to Hudson Bay's ice.

POLAR BEAR

TUNDRA BUGGY

You can take a tour where you sit in a special buggy made to travel over the tundra. It has caged windows so you can get very close to the polar bears. The migration takes place in October or November. The polar bears wait for the waterway to freeze before they start their migration.

WHAT IS THE CLIMATE LIKE IN CANADA?

The people living in Canada have joked that winter goes on for eight months. Then, the remaining four months are needed for road repairs. In many parts of the country, this is true, but Canada is so large that its weather varies a great deal depending on which section of the country you're visiting.

The winters are definitely cold, long, and snowy and in the arctic regions they can be very harsh with daily lows at –20 degrees Fahrenheit. In these areas, there is snow on the ground for about one half of the year and in the far north regions, snow can be seen on the ground for nine months.

In the central and southern regions of the country the summer months get quite hot, so it doesn't always snow in Canada.

VANCOUVER CANADA

SUMMARY

Canada is the second largest country in terms of landmass worldwide, but it is doesn't have much population for its size. Its terrain is a mixture of tall mountains, dense evergreen forests, hilly grasslands, and scenic waterways. Although sections of Canada are cold for nine months of the year, other areas have moderate weather in the spring and hot weather in the summer. The mix of European, native, and other immigrant cultures make Canada unique. There are many natural and manmade attractions to visit if you explore the country of Canada.

Awesome! Now that you've gone exploring in Canada, you may want to visit the country of Poland in the Baby Professor book There's a Lot More than Pretty Windmills in Poland!

Visit
BABY PROFESSOR
EDUCATION KIDS
www.BabyProfessorBooks.com
to download Free Baby Professor eBooks
and view our catalog of new and exciting
Children's Books

www.ingramcontent.com/pod-product-compliance
Lightning Source LLC
Chambersburg PA
CBHW060129120726
48003CB00009B/2821